Original title:
Tales of Tides and Time

Copyright © 2025 Creative Arts Management OÜ
All rights reserved.

Author: Henry Beaumont
ISBN HARDBACK: 978-1-80567-789-5
ISBN PAPERBACK: 978-1-80567-910-3

Currents of Change and Restless Dreams

In a boat made of jelly, I drift and I slide,
The fish wear top hats as they swim side by side.
With seagulls in tutus, it's quite the display,
While crabs throw confetti, on this wavy parade.

I once rode a dolphin, we danced in the sun,
He flipped and he flopped, oh what a wild run!
But then he got tired, and I had to swim,
Now I'm chasing sea turtles with a whim and a grin.

The Landscape of Liquid Time

In a realm where the waves never seem to rest,
A clam claimed he's king; we all found it a jest.
He wore a crown made of seaweed, so proud,
But a tide took it off; his laughter was loud.

When mermaids throw parties, they sing and they sway,
With dolphins as DJs mixing night into day.
When the clock strikes the hour, all fishes must dance,
But a crab's bad breakdancing put folks in a trance.

Siren Songs of the Ebbing Waves

The sirens are crooning; their tunes make fish flip,
A catfish in bow ties can't help but to trip.
With scales that reflect every fanciful note,
They wriggle and giggle, on an old sunken boat.

But be cautious, dear sailors, for glitches may plight,
A lobster with glasses may challenge your sight.
For when songs get too catchy, you might lose the day,
And end up in a clam-shell with naught left to say.

Stories Hidden Beneath the Foam

There's a tale in the bubbles that rise from the sea,
Of a shrimp with big dreams of being a bee.
He buzzed around chirping, but none took a chance,
Until a fish joined in for a ridiculous dance.

As waves crash and tumble, the beachcombers laugh,
Finding shells shaped like hearts and a fish with a scarf.
Their stories entwined in a sea foam embrace,
Life's a big comedy in this watery space.

Time's Gentle Lullaby

The clock ticks loud, a sleepy song,
Dancing shadows, all night long.
Socks on the cat, what a sight!
Dreams of sandwiches take flight.

Nap times come with a gentle plea,
While the goldfish claims the TV.
Tick-tock chaos, such delight,
Jellybeans in every bite.

The Horizon's Forgotten Stories

Seagulls gossip, plotting schemes,
While crabs dance to quirky screams.
Sandcastles made with a sneaky grin,
And a lost flip-flop keeps the win.

A whale hums a tale of the day,
Of fish who jive, come what may.
With a splash and a wink, they twirl,
Underwater blues in a whirl.

Beneath the Surface: Stories Untold

Octopus dreams of being a chef,
Stirring the sea with a noodle bereft.
Clams hold secrets, pearls they boast,
But they can never finish their toast.

Fish with hats swim by the reef,
As seahorses share tales of belief.
Bubble-wrap laughter fills the waves,
And jellyfish do the floss, like raves.

Whirlpools of Yesterday

History swims in a whirlpool spin,
With rubber duckies wearing a grin.
Sailors lost on jelly bean shores,
Searching for treasure and candy galores.

Mermaids giggle, splashing with glee,
As pirates juggle underwater tea.
Each wave carries jokes like flotsam,
In the sea of laughter, we're all welcome.

Timeless Horizons of the Soul

On a ship made of jellybeans,
We sailed through skies of blue.
The captain was a dancing bear,
And the crew just laughed, it's true.

With lollipops for anchors strong,
We drifted past the clouds so high.
Each wave a giggle, every splash,
Was just our snacks falling by.

The sun wore sunglasses of ice cream,
As we dipped our toes in candy seas.
Time forgot to take a break,
While the breeze told jokes with ease.

So here we are, with dreams alight,
Riding rainbows, feeling fine.
We sail on whims, in silly glee,
For sea and soul are truly mine.

Promises Carried by the Winds

The wind whistled tunes of laughter,
As we raced a kite in the park.
It zoomed and zigzagged like a dancer,
Singing tales until it got dark.

With whispers of secrets in our ears,
We promised to chase the heights.
But the wind, being quite mischievous,
Wrapped our kite in the nearby lights.

Oh, how we rolled on the grass,
Laughing till our cheeks turned red.
For every twist the wind unraveled,
Was just more giggles overhead.

As dusk painted hues of orange and gold,
We knew the wind's tricks were bright.
With friends by our side, we'd soar and glide,
In the magic of this playful night.

Saltwater Memories and Moon Dancers

At the beach, we found a sand crab,
Dancing like it owned the shore.
With each twist, it made us giggle,
We clapped and dubbed it 'King of Lore.'

The waves painted whispers on our feet,
As we danced in the salty spray.
With every splash, we shared a laugh,
And let all our worries float away.

A moonbeam stuck in a fisherman's hat,
Made the night feel bright and bold.
We wiggled our toes with the tides,
Creating stories that never get old.

So let the sea be our storyteller,
As stars flicker in the sky's embrace.
We'll take our saltwater memories,
And dance like crabs in this carefree space.

Legends Swayed by the Wind's Voice

Once there was a goofy old tree,
That could tell tales, but forgot.
Its branches waved like silly arms,
As it danced with each breeze—it was hot!

The birds perched near, quite perplexed,
As they listened to its nonsense lore.
"Twinkle toes!" it shouted in joy,
"Could someone please unlock the door?"

We gathered round, curious and keen,
With popcorn kernels in our bags.
For every gust, the stories grew,
Mixing giggles with the flags.

The moon winked down, bemused by all,
As the wind whirled and swayed it true.
In the forest's heart, it just made sense,
For laughter was the best view.

The Shift in the Celestial Tide

The moon forgot its nightly show,
Dancing high, then tripping low.
Stars giggled in the darkened sea,
As jellyfish swam on a cup of tea.

The sun wore shades, a beachy vibe,
While waves made jokes, all slick and sly.
Seagulls laughed, a raucous cheer,
As tides played tag, drawing near.

Crabs played cards on sandy chairs,
Shells were caps, no signs of cares.
Fish told tales of fishy fright,
While clams clacked jokes, oh what a sight!

In this frolicking watery glow,
Time forgot, as currents flow.
With giggles swirling, life was grand,
In a world where laughter ruled the sand.

Chronicles of a Withering Cliff

Once stood a cliff so proud and tall,
Now it leans, a slumping sprawl.
Seagulls perched, a watchful crew,
Chortling at the view anew.

Pebbles chat, 'What a steep descent!'
'Can we get a lift?' one pebble bent.
A rock said, 'I'm here for a laugh,
Watching you roll, what a rough path!'

The breeze shared secrets, soft and gruff,
'This cliff won't budge—he's had enough!'
Against the waves, it makes its stand,
While whispers of erosion grace the land.

Yet every tumble ignites a jest,
As nature's humor puts 'time' to rest.
With cracks and chuckles, and hair made of moss,
Our cliff might crumble, but no need to toss!

Legacy of the Forgotten Ocean

In a sea of socks and lost odd shoes,
The fishes giggle, with nothing to lose.
Drifting amidst the bubbles and fluff,
Seaweed holds court, calling all bluff.

'Remember when tides were grand and wide?
Now we're surfing on nets that slide!'
A whale cracked jokes, 'I'll take a sip,
Of lemonade from a sinking ship!'

Coral reefs, with their colorful attire,
Throw glitter parties, never to tire.
With every wave, a splash of wit,
A mermaid's wink, folks just don't quit!

In this realm of whimsical sea lore,
Laughter bubbles up from the ocean floor.
Through sunken treasures and tales unwritten,
A legacy blooms, while silly jokes are smitten.

Whirlpools of Yesterday

Spinning circles of water and glee,
Whirlpools sipping tea quite carefree.
Round and round in a playful whine,
As ducks play duck-duck-goose, just divine!

Pirates lost in swirling spins,
Concocting schemes with grins and pins.
'Where's the treasure?' a parrot squawked,
While seaweed giggled, silhouettes mocked.

Yesterday's tides, they hold their fun,
Reminiscing tales, they've just begun.
With playful currents, they weave and wind,
A dance with the waves, unconfined.

And as they swirl with laughter and cheer,
The ripples echo, 'Time's not here!'
For in this whirlpool of jokes afloat,
Life drifts merrily, in a silly boat.

Whispers of the Endless Waves

The seaweed sings a silly tune,
As crabs do the cha-cha under the moon.
Seagulls squawk, they think they're grand,
While barnacles conspire on the sand.

Oh look! A wave with a big belly laugh,
Knocking down shells like it's a quick gaffe.
Fish do flips, oh what a sight,
In the ocean's party, all through the night.

Echoes from the Shoreline

The beachball bounces, it thinks it's a star,
While flip-flops race, becoming bizarre.
A towel whispers secrets of sunburn fears,
As kids throw tantrums, while squaring off with cheers.

The shells gossip, oh what a fuss!
Saying, 'Who invited that sandy bus?'
Waves keep rolling, with stories to share,
While crabs throw a dance party in the air.

Sandcastles in the Moonlight

A castle of sand, with moats made of cheese,
Waves crashing softly, saying 'Please don't tease!'
The knight, a seagull, with a shell for a sword,
Squawks at the sea, while the mermaids hoard.

With turrets of sand, and a drawbridge of drift,
The tide waves goodbye, what a goofy gift!
Sandfly the brave fights the sea breeze and wins,
While starfish celebrate with their silly fins.

Currents of Memory

A stick floats by, pretending to sail,
While jellyfish wiggle, spinning a tale.
Old flip-flops reminisce in the brine,
As the tide plays tag—'What's yours is now mine!'

The fish toss jokes, in bubbles they giggle,
At the silly old crabs who just love to wiggle.
Seashells collect whispers from days gone past,
In currents of laughter, may the fun last!

Echoes of a Forgotten Seaway

There once was a fish named Lou,
Who dreamed of a life in a shoe.
He swam past a crab,
With a hat and a jab,
And said, "Join me for some ocean stew!"

Old sailors would tell tales of whales,
Who danced with the wind and the gales.
They'd laugh till they cried,
As the waves rolled wide,
While seagulls were stealing their pails!

A lobster once wanted to fly,
He strapped on some wings, oh my!
He soared through the air,
With a slight bit of flair,
Till a seagull said, "You'll just fry!"

So now in the sea where they be,
The creatures live wild and carefree.
With bubbles and jest,
They laugh with the best,
In their underwater jubilee!

Celestial Currents and Memory's Embrace

The moon had a party one night,
With starfish that twinkled so bright.
They waltzed on the waves,
Like graceful knaves,
In a dance that felt just right!

A comet came zipping through the sky,
Asked a jellyfish, "Wanna try?"
They whirled and they spun,
Had an ocean of fun,
Till the jelly said, "Oh, I think I'll cry!"

The tides played the tunes of the sea,
As the dolphins joined in with glee.
With flips and with flops,
They made funny hops,
And shared all their finest esprit!

Through bubbles of laughter and light,
Was a world full of joy and delight.
Each splash and each cheer,
Brought the ocean near,
In a harmony that felt just right!

Landscapes Crafted by Ocean's Breath

A crab built a castle of sand,
He claimed it was quite rather grand.
But each time it would rain,
He'd frown with disdain,
As it washed away all he had planned.

An octopus wanted to paint,
With colors that simply would faint.
He splattered the brine,
With shades quite divine,
But ended up looking like a saint!

The seashells had parties each week,
In outfits that made them unique.
That clam wore a crown,
With pearls all around,
While the mussels played hide-and-seek!

So here in the swell of the sea,
Where the laughter and antics run free,
The creatures will cheer,
With a splash and a sneer,
In their vibrant aquatic jubilee!

Rippling Reflections of Eternity

The fish all gather for their daily chat,
Gossiping 'bout the dog that's gone quite fat.
A turtle's slow dance makes the seaweed twirl,
While starfish practices its aerial whirl.

The crabs wear hats made of seagrass chic,
Waving their claws, they say, "Take a peek!"
A jellyfish moonwalks, a sight to see,
Mixing fashion with a splash of glee.

As currents giggle, tides tickle the shore,
The seagulls crack jokes, oh, they ask for more!
The sea otters hold a weekly dance-off,
Their synchronized moves make the big waves scoff.

When mermaids tell stories, the dolphins cheer,
"All aboard! Time to swim, our boat's right here!"
With laughter echoing through the salty air,
They revel in currents, bringing joy everywhere.

Muted Words of the Distant Shore

A clam's witty quips just grow more absurd,
Its shell's a safe space, but oh, how it's heard!
The octopus juggles with shells and a smile,
While sea cucumbers lounge, making it worthwhile.

The sandcastles boast of their towering might,
But crabs dig tunnels, soon out of sight.
Waves roll in whispers, like secrets they keep,
But the seagulls squawk loud, never letting us sleep.

As tides pull the seaweed, it dances with flair,
And worries dissolve in the salty sea air.
The fish wear sunglasses, reclining with ease,
While barnacles gossip, their tales never freeze.

As twilight descends, the stars start to glow,
The sea sparkles back with a performance show.
With a wink and a wave, the night slips away,
And tomorrow they'll start with a sunlit display.

Where Time Meets the Ocean Floor

Time takes a dive, and fishes start to race,
While corals chuckle in this watery space.
A dolphin complains, "Why swim all day?"
But the turtles just say, "We're living the play!"

Starfish share gossips about the sea snails,
While clumsy old crabs are telling tall tales.
The petals of kelps brush the seabed with grace,
As urchins laugh softly, it's a joyful place.

Seashells exchange stories of treasures untold,
While waves weave around them in threads of gold.
The whole ocean's chuckling, no reason to pout,
For this world's full of wonders; that's what it's about.

"Catch me if you can!" the silver fish tease,
While jellybeans bounce with a bloop and a breeze.
As time swirls away, bringing laughter galore,
The ocean's a playground, forever we'll explore!

Lullabies of the Illusive Sea

The waves croon softly, a playful request,
"Join us for a slumber, it's truly the best!"
Anemones sway while the sea stars hum,
While otters drift off, their dreams are so fun.

A sleepy blue whale croons its lullaby,
While plankton tango underneath the night sky.
The shells on the beach tell stories they know,
Of pirates and treasures buried below.

As the moonlight twinkles on rippling waves,
Fishies hold hands and do everything brave.
They whisper sweet secrets in currents that glide,
As laughter and sleep intertwine on the tide.

So drift with the rhythm, let worries all cease,
In the heart of the ocean, find comfort and peace.
With dreams that are vast and tales spun with glee,
The deep whispering lullabies of the sea.

A Canvas of Stars and Seafoam

Bubbles burst on sandy shores,
Seagulls laugh in seaside stores.
Crabs wear hats of seaweed green,
Playing tag, a funny scene.

Starfish dance in sandy boots,
While fish sing with funny flutes.
Tide pools wink with cheeky grins,
As shells share their sandy sins.

Whispers of the Ocean's Embrace

The ocean's breath whispers a joke,
Seashells giggle, and corals poke.
Waves tickle toes, a splashy prank,
Dolphins dive with a playful plank.

Mermaids chuckle, tails in knots,
With seaweed wigs and forgotten thoughts.
Each wave's a wink, a twist, a tease,
Nature's dance of laughter and ease.

Echoes Beneath the Distant Waves

Beneath the surface, fish convene,
Telling tales with flippered sheen.
Octopuses juggle, quite absurd,
While starfish giggle, not a word.

Remarkable crabs with secret shrugs,
Share their snacks, and hug the plugs.
A sea cucumber rolls with glee,
In this underwater comedy.

The Hourglass of Endless Shores

Time ticks away in a sandy jar,
While sea turtles ponder how far.
Shellfish gossip, plotting mischief,
With tides that hold a playful whiff.

Sandcastles grow with wonky towers,
While kids giggle through sunny hours.
An hourglass spilling giggle and fun,
As shadows stretch beneath the sun.

The Dance of Sea and Sky

The waves waltz up and down,
The gulls are the clumsy clowns.
Seagulls dive for fish with glee,
While the ocean tickles their feet.

A starfish in a top hat spins,
Crabs clack their claws, join the din.
The lighthouse shines a disco ball,
Shells join in the groove, oh so tall.

The sun slips in, a cheeky grin,
Making waves dance, let's all begin.
The breeze plays tune, a feathery tune,
As jellyfish glide in a jubilant swoon.

But as night falls, the show must end,
A fish waves goodbye to a gloomy friend.
The sea yawns wide, the sky salutes,
Tomorrow's dance shall bear new hoots.

Lanterns of the Rising Sun

Bright krill twirl in morning's glow,
Like tiny lanterns in a row.
The sun peeks out, a wink so sly,
While fish flash scales, oh my, oh my!

A crab with shades walks with a strut,
While turtles gossip, 'What's in that rut?'
The seaweed sways, it knows the beat,
As shrimp do cha-cha with some pep in their feet.

As clams chirp, 'Good morning, world!'
An octopus juggles pearls, twirled!
The dolphins leap, a joyous spree,
Inviting all shells to join—yippee!

The glowing sun beams down with cheer,
While the ocean chuckles, 'Come near, my dear!'
From dawn to dusk, laughter in streams,
A chorus of bubbles and happy dreams.

Chronicles of the Ocean's Heart

Once a fish wore a sparkly hat,
It claimed to be the king of that.
But a dolphin swirled in for a chat,
'Hey there buddy, how about that?'

The octopus scribbled tales of fame,
On seaweed scrolls, it played the game.
But one wrong poke led to a splash,
As clowns in the reef began to crash!

Anemones knitted tales so strange,
Of turtles that rapped and feasted on change.
With wriggly tales, the giggles spread,
While sea stars danced on the tales they read.

But watch out, as the tide chimes clear,
For every tale fades when you persevere.
In the ocean's heart, that playful art,
Echoes a laugh—a light-hearted part!

Celestial Waves and Silent Shores

The moon waves hello with a cheeky pose,
While waves giggle softly, tickling toes.
A starfish whispered, 'Wish for a ride,'
But jelly replied, 'Please, not that side!'

The beach ball bobbed like a happy seal,
And crabs marched round with a rhythm to feel.
Sandcastles crumbled, a soft giggle burst,
Life in the waves, oh how to quench thirst!

A seahorse dances in a conga line,
While sea cucumbers say, 'We're divine!'
The tides huddle in a wagon of dreams,
As seashells chat in a chorus of gleams.

When twilight whispers on darkened waves,
The ocean chuckles, its heart still braves.
In silence, it hums, a lively score,
Casting out laughter on the echoing shore.

Ghosts of the Sailor's Past

The old sailor swears he saw,
A fish in boots, a sight of awe.
It danced a jig upon the deck,
And knocked the captain's rum, what the heck!

A parrot squawked with salty glee,
'There's treasure here, just wait and see!'
But when they dug, they found a shoe,
And laughed so hard, their sides just flew!

The ghost of mermaids sang their song,
About a ship that sailed so wrong.
With every wave, a tale so bold,
Of plundered snacks and secrets told.

So raise a toast to every ghost,
Who haunts the sea and loves it most.
For in their tales, both strange and bright,
The ocean's laughs will bring delight!

The Promise of Distant Shores

The seagulls squawk amidst the breeze,
A hint of laughter in the trees.
With nets of dreams, the sailors roam,
In search of fish that might call home.

A map of crumbs leads them afar,
To distant lands and a coconut jar.
Yet every time they find a treat,
It's just a crab who wants to eat!

The promise of shores where fun is found,
Where jellybeans rain down, unbound.
Yet every wave brings silly strife,
As they bump into a jellyfish life!

So here's to sailing, wild and free,
With laughter echoing on the sea.
For every prank and every cheer,
Brings endless joy to those who steer!

Ink of the Waters: A Love Letter

With waves that wink, a heart did send,
A bottle of love, a seashell friend.
The ink was squid, oh what a mess,
But that's just how love's meant to express!

Across the shores, the letter flew,
A seahorse read it, feeling blue.
It curled it tight and sighed with grace,
Wishing for a just fishy embrace!

But when the tides did roll and sway,
The letter flipped and danced away.
The love now lost, but surely not,
For fishy hearts can share a thought!

So toss your dreams upon the sea,
And write your love, wild and free.
For in each wave and splash so bright,
Is ink of waters, pure delight!

The Clockwork of the Ocean

Tick-tock, the ocean chimes,
With dancing clocks and salty rhymes.
The fish all wear their finest gear,
And waltz around, the time is near!

A crab with glasses peered so wise,
Claimed time was just a fishy guise.
He ticked and tocked and laughed quite loud,
Beneath the waves, he drew a crowd!

With starfish hands that waved in tune,
They made a clock beneath the moon.
Yet every time the hand would spin,
A dolphin leaped, proclaiming sin!

So let's embrace this silly spree,
Where time is just a jamboree.
With ocean clocks and rhymes galore,
The clockwork sea will ever roar!

The Pulse of Distant Horizons

On sandy shores, a crab took flight,
It stole my sandwich in broad daylight.
With a flip and a scuttle, it danced away,
Leaving me munching on seaweed parfait.

The seagulls squawked, they eyed my pie,
As waves laughed hard, oh my, oh my!
A lighthouse winked, playing peek-a-boo,
While the ocean's tune hummed a silly blue.

My flip-flops flopped like fish out of school,
With each goofy step, I felt quite the fool.
But laughter echoed where seagrass sways,
As I tripped with grace on these sandy bays.

Riptides of Recollection

Oh, the riptides whisk away days of yore,
When I tried to surf and fell right ashore.
Each tumble and splash brought laughter galore,
As my friends on the beach called for more and more.

An octopus waved, my biggest fan,
While a dolphin danced, that slick little span.
With my board in hand and sand in my hair,
I crafted a legend of pirate despair.

As seagulls snickered and the waves would tease,
I rolled like a log, just doing that sneeze.
Time spun like seashells, away from the clock,
Each moment a giggle, each wave was a knock.

Forgotten Shores and Shifting Skies

On forgotten shores where flip-flops lay,
A starfish wore shades, it stole the display.
With a wink and a wave, it silently gloated,
Claiming my towel, oh they've really exploded!

The sun slouched low, like a tired old man,
As I sang to the gulls, my forgotten plan.
With each shifting sky, more colors did scream,
Like a tie-dye explosion, a surreal daydream.

A crab in a bowtie joined the soirée,
With a conch for a mic, it stole the bouquet.
Together we danced, though only half right,
While the ocean chuckled, under the light.

Chronicles Written in the Surf

In frothy waves, my stories unfurl,
Each bubble a dream, each splash a twirl.
The seafoam giggled, 'Write your best lines,'
As I conjured up mermaids sipping on wines.

They tossed me a fish that twirled like a pro,
While crabs clapped their claws, putting on a show.
A dolphin named Gary high-fived my head,
As I crafted my tale in this sandy thread.

With every new wave, my laughter did swell,
The surf became pages, oh can you tell?
From shores to the sky, where nonsense is king,
The sea is a scribe, of folly it sings.

The Passage of Sunlit Waters

The fish wore hats, quite in style,
They danced in circles, with a smile.
A crab with glasses read the news,
While seashells giggled in fancy shoes.

The sunbeams twirled, playing tag,
A dolphin raced, just to brag.
But waves were sneaky, oh so sly,
They splashed the seagulls, who cried goodbye.

The turtles joined, they brought a snack,
With jellybeans tucked in their pack.
The octopus served drinks with flair,
As beach balls floated high in air.

But just as fun was set to peak,
In swam a whale who couldn't speak.
He tried to dance, but oh dear me!
A slip, a slide, and off went he!

Secrets Buried in Driftwood

A log sat proud upon the shore,
Claiming treasure, just folklore.
It whispered tales to passing snails,
Of pirate gold and ghostly gales.

But hidden there, oh what a sight!
A rubber duck took off in flight.
With beady eyes and a wink so bright,
It honked with glee at the dusk's last light.

The seagulls laughed, they took their bets,
On who could catch what they called nets.
While crabs held court on sandy thrones,
Beneath driftwood, they shared funny tones.

In evening's glow, tales spun and twined,
A mermaid swam with fishing line.
For every secret, every riddle,
Was just the ocean's playful middle.

The Cycle of Resting Stars

At dusk, the stars put on their hats,
While planets giggled with the cats.
They took a break, laid back with ease,
As comets danced, just like the breeze.

One star blushed, so shy and sweet,
While meteors tried to catch a beat.
From here to there, a swirling dream,
Lights twinkled softly, like a gleam.

A cluster formed a funny crew,
They told jokes as the night flew.
The moon rolled by, quite full of cheer,
But tripped on stardust, oh dear, oh dear!

They laughed till dawn peeked with a grin,
As sunbeams stretched their arms to win.
And stars, with chuckles wide and bright,
Fell asleep, to rest till night.

Harmony in the Rustling Tides

The waves practiced tunes, like a band so slick,
While seashells clapped, picking up the kick.
A sea cucumber strummed a guitar,
As fish formed a line, swaying near and far.

The jellyfish boogied and spun with flair,
While seaweed danced without a care.
They twirled in rhythm, a fluid flight,
As bubbles popped in the morning light.

But wait! A crab with two left feet,
Joined the conga, now that was neat!
He tripped on coral, fell into a pout,
But the dolphins cheered, "Come on, don't pout!"

Together they laughed till the tides gave way,
With flippers and fins, they brightened the day.
In harmony, they sang through salty air,
For in the ocean, fun is everywhere!

Secrets of Salt and Sand

A crab in a tux, what a sight!
Dancing on the beach, oh what a fright!
Seagulls cackle, calling a friend,
While sneaky waves plot a splashy end.

Shells whisper secrets from long ago,
Of mermaids who danced with a mystical glow.
A bucket gets kicked, wet shoes take flight,
As sandcastles crumble with all of their might.

The tide has a laugh, low tide, high tide,
Swirling and twirling like a merry ride.
An octopus juggles, seaweed in hand,
While kids giggle, forming a band.

So grab your flip-flops, let's wade in the foam,
Where laughter and joy find a home.
With salt in the air and sunshine so grand,
We'll chase all the giggles across the warm sand.

Currents of Memory in Motion

Floating on memories, just drifting along,
An otter sings out its favorite song.
With seaweed as a scarf, oh so chic,
It twirls and spins—such a silly peak!

The tide pulls us back, then pushes us forth,
Like rubber duckies making their worth.
Each wave a punchline, each splash a pun,
Cracking up whales who just want some fun.

A jellyfish blooms, kind of a sight,
With tentacles twirling in pure delight.
It winks at the fish while they giggle and dart,
Creating a wave that's more swipe than art.

Rivers wrap stories in bubbles so bright,
Swirling in laughter from morning to night.
So let's ride the currents, let's not resist,
In a sea full of memories, you surely can't miss.

The Rhythm of the Rising Bay

The bay has a beat, a whimsical sound,
With clams doing cha-chas right out of the ground.
Flipping and flopping, they dance with glee,
While waves tap their feet, oh what a spree!

Pelicans dive with a splash and a show,
While starfish grin wide, just go with the flow.
Sunshine twinkles on water like stars,
As shells crack jokes from their sandy bars.

A dolphin makes waves with jokes from the deep,
Pulling up pranks that make others leap.
With a twist and a flip, he steals the scene,
While crabs clap their claws—what a fun routine!

So let the tides lead us on this bright ride,
With laughter and joy by the sparkling side.
We'll sway with the rhythm, forever entwined,
In the lively embrace of the ocean's great mind.

Sands Through the Hourglass

In an hourglass, sands are in play,
Critters celebrate, come dance and sway!
Time's a prankster, it runs and it skips,
With pirates and mermaids making odd quips.

An old watch tells tales of a clumsy old crab,
Who tripped on his claws while trying to grab.
With grains straying out, they whisper of fun,
As the sun paints the sky, laughing, just one.

This hourglass spins, round and round it goes,
Giving sea creatures their time to pose.
With a wink and a nod, they all agree,
That laughing in sand is the best way to be!

So flip it around, let the fun come alive,
With shells spinning stories of joy—oh, they thrive!
Time flows like the waves, in a dance so divine,
In the sands of life, all of us shine.

Chronicles of Swells and Whispers

Once a wave tried to tickle a boat,
But the boat just wobbled and fell, oh what a note!
Seagulls laughed, they couldn't believe,
The ocean's antics were hard to conceive.

A crab told a joke, but it pinched too hard,
The fish rolled their eyes, it was quite a shard.
The sand laughed so loud, it danced with glee,
While starfish yawned, 'Let it be, let it be.'

A dolphin slipped in with a splashy grin,
Said, "I'm the king of the wave, let's begin!"
The turtles groaned, 'Not this again!'
While the shrimp just grooved in their elegant pen.

So gather your tales at the shore's wide span,
With laughter and bubbles, it's a wild clan.
From squawks to splashes, let the fun times flow,
In the kingdom of sea, where hilarity grows.

The Song of the Lapping Waves

The lapping waves sing a bubbly tune,
Whispers of mischief beneath the warm moon.
A fish in a hat did wiggle and sway,
"I'm the best dancer, just watch me play!"

A seal with a wink, tried to do the twist,
"I'm on the cover of 'Ocean's Top List!'"
But he slipped and flopped, making a splash,
The seaweed laughed hard, oh what a crash!

Two crabs in a race forgot where to go,
Caught up in gossip, as tides start to flow.
With a flick and a flip, they raced to the end,
Only to find that the sea had no bend.

In this frothy world, where giggles abound,
Seashells echo the chuckles all around.
So join in the song, let your laughter prevail,
With the lapping waves, life's one grand tale.

When Time Dances with the Sea

Time dressed like a pirate, eye-patch and all,
Stumbled on deck and began to enthrall.
The waves spun around, so caught in the jive,
Even barnacles smiled, feeling alive!

"Dance with me, time!" called a cheeky old boat,
But time tripped on a rope and nearly went afloat.
The buoys giggled softly, "What a sight to see!"
"Oh dear!" said the dolphins, "Is this meant to be?"

A clock with a smile joined in for the fun,
Tick-tocked to the rhythm, oh wasn't it run?
The shells clapped along, lost in the beat,
While waves kept on dancing, not missing a seat.

When time scoffs and shimmies, remember the lore,
For laughter's the treasure washed up on the shore.
So join in this waltz, where the sea meets the skies,
In a world where the minutes dance, oh what a surprise!

Glimmers of Time on the Horizon

The sun dipped low, casting glimmers of fun,
While clams did a tango, oh weren't they spun!
A whale in a tuxedo played games on the strand,
With a wink and a nod, he took off his band.

Seagulls took bets on which fish would win,
As crabs held a contest, a real cheeky spin.
Time floated by in a bubblegum boat,
With laughs and splashes, the good times would gloat.

A message in a bottle, tossed by the waves,
Said, "Join the party, you silly knaves!"
So starfish embraced, with sandcastles tall,
Creating a kingdom with laughter for all.

In the glimmers of time, where memories last,
The horizon echoed with chuckles from the past.
So take a dive in the fun, don't delay,
For every ripple sings, 'What a wacky day!'

The Rhythm of Water's Embrace

When the waves crash, I slip and slide,
In my flip-flops, I take a wild ride.
Seagulls squawk, dive-bomb my snack,
I duck for cover, then launch my attack.

Buckets of water, splashing all around,
Frolicking friends in a laughter sound.
Sunburned noses, and sand in my hair,
A dance with the sea, free without care.

Shells and driftwood, treasures galore,
A crab makes a run for the next sandy door.
We chase it down, we're laughing with glee,
Who knew that a beach could be so carefree?

The tide rolls in, bringing salt and cheer,
With each splash, I raise my cup of beer.
To the ocean's tune, we sing and we sway,
Life's a beach, who needs to be gray?

Ebb and Flow: A Journey

The sea pulls back, like a game of tag,
We dance in circles, it makes us gag.
Sandy feet and giggles fill the day,
We build a castle, until it gives way.

Crabs in tuxedos, prance by my side,
While jellyfish float by with nowhere to hide.
With each little splash, laughter takes flight,
In a world where everything feels just right.

My friend slips down, into the blue sea,
Flailing like a fish, oh let him be!
Waterlogged pants, a sight to behold,
We roll on the sand, laughing uncontrolled.

As night falls gently, the waves start to hum,
Stars begin twinkling - it's a cosmic drum.
We wave goodbye to this wonderful place,
With grains of sand, sparkling on our face.

Secrets Beneath the Horizon

What lurks beneath, we all want to see,
A fish in a tux? Or maybe a flea?
With snorkels on, we dive down for a peek,
Only to find, a rusted old leak.

Octopus floating, wearing a hat,
Cosmic sea urchins, all dressed in sprat.
Little fish giggle, all swimming around,
In this underwater circus, joy is found.

The mermaid's lost pearl? We think we might find,
But all we uncover is a treasure of twine.
A round fish swims by, he steals the show,
With moves like a dancer, oh don't be slow!

Up to the surface, we surface with cheer,
Full of giggles and stories to share here.
What's better than laughter, and friends to adore?
Underwater secrets, we couldn't ask for more!

Driftwood Dreams and Distant Stars

Driftwood dreams whisper tales in my ear,
Of floating logs and a sky full of cheer.
With wishes like stars, we send them to sea,
Hoping they bounce back, just funny like me.

In the distance, a ship sails loony tunes,
With a captain who strums on his ukulele moons.
"Ahoy there!" we shout, with a big toothy grin,
And dance with the waves, let the laughter begin!

Under the moonlight, we gather 'round tight,
Driftwood and campfire, what a magical sight!
Marshmallows roasting, they puff up so round,
We chase them with laughter, 'til they hit the ground.

With dusk creeping in, our dreams take to flight,
As the sky unveils wonders, pure sparkles of light.
Hand in hand, we wander the shore's playful beams,
In driftwood's embrace, we build all our dreams.

Moonlit Dances on the Water's Edge

Under a moon that bathes the shore,
Crabs do the conga, oh, but there's more!
Seagulls in tuxedos, flapping their wings,
Dancing with jellyfish, oh the joy it brings.

The sand's our stage, the ocean's our tune,
Shells clapping loudly, they'll rattle your spoon!
The starfish are judges, all laughing with glee,
As dolphins twist prologs, 'Look at me, look at me!'

But wait for the tide, it has other plans,
Sweeping away the best dancer's pants!
With a splash and a spray, the waves crash the show,
In this watery bash, everyone ought to go!

As night slips away, all the critters retreat,
Leaving behind only leftover seaweed treats.
So gather your shells, and don't be a bore,
Join the moonlit dance, and let your heart soar!

Refugees of the Forgotten Currents

Fish in bow ties, lost in a stream,
Their travel plans wasted, they lost the last dream.
Floating on debris from ships long ago,
With seashells as baggage, they put on a show.

A snail in a fedora, sings tales in a whirl,
While crabs clutch their cocktails, and give a twirl.
The sea turtle's a bouncer, keeping the peace,
Ensuring lost travelers get some release.

But here comes the tide, with a mischievous grin,
Snatching our fish from the hull's scoff and din.
Up on a wave they ride like a kite,
Each splash is a tale of their endless flight.

In this wacky adventure, slowly unwinds,
Are fish more than travelers or simply unkind?
With laughter and glee, they chase off the gloom,
As seaweed confetti bursts out in a plume!

Beneath the Surface of a Timeless Sea

Bubbles are giggling, oh what a sight,
An octopus juggling, with all of his might.
Sea urchins are cheering, they float to the beat,
As fish flash their smiles, all swimming in heat.

A clam tells a story, oh what a twist,
Of turtles wearing top hats, how could we resist?
Crabs crafting krusty jokes, making us snort,
While mermaids add sass, in the underwater court.

But just then a wave comes, with all of its force,
Every fish and creature made a mad course!
They swirl and they spin, in a dizzying way,
As the ocean chuckles, 'Hey, join our ballet!'

And though they all tire, with glowing bright eyes,
They trust the sea currents, and rise to the skies.
In laughter and joy, they push back the night,
For under the waves, there's always delight!

The Dance of Waves and Whispers

The waves clap their hands, as they swirl and twirl,
With whispers of seashells, a sparkly whirl.
They giggle like toddlers, splashing the breeze,
While fish flip in rhythm, making seaweed tease.

A wave tossed a comet, but look, here it fell,
And landed right smack on a pufferfish's shell.
With laughter erupting, they all sang a tune,
'Oh, floating through space? Now that's quite the boon!'

They swayed back and forth, in a flowing parade,
As bubbles burst forth, in delight they cascaded.
A frog on a lily, sipping a drink,
Shouted, "I love water! Come join the wink!"

With giggles and splashes, they all held a toast,
To the creatures of sea, and the friends they love most.
As the tide carries on, with a wink and a nod,
In this dance of the waves, there's no reason to plod!

In the Wake of Shifting Sands

The crab wore boots, quite stylish too,
He danced a jig, what a silly view!
Seagulls squawked, with hats askew,
While waves whispered secrets, oh if they knew!

A starfish twirled on the ocean floor,
With jellyfish friends, they looked to the shore.
They chuckled and giggled, what a fun score,
Creating a splash, always wanting more!

A sandcastle built, it rose oh so high,
But a rogue wave crashed, made it say goodbye.
The sandman laughed as he waved a sly tie,
While the beach ball rolled, with a merry bye-bye!

Eels in sunglasses, pretending to tan,
While fish on surfboards devised a great plan.
The tide rolls in, making everyone fan,
As the ocean's antics became quite the clan!

Recollections in Tidal Flow

A whale with a hat sang a tune so sweet,
While dolphins performed, light on their feet.
Mermaids giggled, oh what a treat,
As the bubbles burst, laughter couldn't be beat!

The tide played tricks, making shells dance,
Crabs in a conga, caught in a trance.
They twirled in the foam, oh what a chance,
To spin and to laugh with a playful glance!

A clam with a pearl had a story to share,
How he once dated a fish, quite a rare pair.
They laughed 'til they cried, floating free in the air,
While the seaweed swayed without a care!

The current carried a joke, quite absurd,
About a fish who liked to wear a bird.
With every wave, the laughter stirred,
Echoing tales that were never disturbed!

Enigmas of the Ebbing Sea

A wise old octopus counted the stars,
On an old rusty boat, with a dash of bizarre.
He spun silly riddles, like hidden memoirs,
While seashells debated their favorite bars!

Fish in tuxedos swam with great flair,
They practiced their moves with elegant care.
The squids juggled bubbles, floating in air,
As crabs cracked jokes about who's unfair!

The tide took a footrace with the bright moon,
But the sea breeze cheered, saying, "Not so soon!"
As barnacles chuckled, humming a tune,
Life on the coastline was never a swoon!

A treasure chest opened, not gold but some socks,
What a delight for the curious flocks!
Seagulls squawked stories that left us in shocks,
As the ocean conspired to play with the clocks!

Interludes of the Endless Blue

Seashells conspired, plotting a game,
With crabs as their players, nobody was tame.
They laughed when the tide tossed a splash of fame,
What a spectacle, oh isn't it lame?

A pelican perched, surveying the scene,
Saw a fish wearing glasses, looking quite keen.
With a wink and a nod, what a sight to glean,
The antics of friends under skies of marine!

Tiny turtles raced, slow but so sly,
With seaweed as flags, they waved goodbye.
The waves cheered them on, oh how time did fly,
As the sun set low, painting worlds in the sky!

Anemones giggled, tickled by the sway,
While the tides told riddles in their own way.
With laughter and joy, they danced through the spray,
In this endless blue, where fun finds its play!

Timelines Etched in Coral Hearts

In a world where fish wear shoes,
And crabs paint murals, bold and bright,
They argue who's the best at blues,
While dolphins giggle at the sight.

Clams hold court on ocean floors,
Claiming they're the king of bling,
But all they do is close their doors,
And miss the waves of what life brings.

Seahorses dance to tunes of old,
While octopuses play hide and seek,
With tales of treasure yet untold,
In waves, they splutter, laugh and squeak.

So join this joyous, salty crew,
Where laughter bubbles, never ends,
In every wave, a joke rings true,
As time winks back, and silliness transcends.

Beneath the Surface of a Brimming Tide

Bubbles float in the sunny sea,
As sea turtles try to do ballet,
They wobble, splutter, laugh with glee,
While anchovies just joke and play.

The starfish all are quite the jesters,
With arms outstretched, they wave hello,
But they're just stuck, much like the rest here,
And grumble, wishing they could go.

A blowfish tells a terrible pun,
While clowns of the reef just roll their eyes,
As waves dance up and down for fun,
Encouraging laughter 'neath bright skies.

So dive down deep, don't be confined,
Surfacing with joy, not dread,
For ocean's humor is unrefined,
And bubbles pop with every spread.

The Ancient Questions of the Sea

Why do whales always sing so loud?
Is it to tickle fish, or is it charm?
The jellyfish are lost in their shroud,
Wobbling along, free from alarm.

Why do sharks wear such grumpy frowns?
When dolphins splash and leap with flair,
And seagulls swoop down, stealing crowns,
While crabs look on, quite unaware.

Do mermaids really brush their hair?
With seashells and pearls, it seems so grand,
But lost between the salty air,
It's just another fishy band.

So if you ponder, take a dive,
With ocean's laughter as your guide,
In churning waves, the truth will thrive,
And searching hearts will turn with pride.

When Echoes Meet Endless Water

At dawn, the sea whispers its jokes,
To shells and rocks, it tickles the shore,
The laughter echoes out like pokes,
As waves come crashing, wanting more.

The sand crabs gossip about old ships,
Who's heard the tales of treasures, fake?
While gulls just eye with flapping lips,
And dive right into a sneaky break.

Starry nights reveal moonlit pranks,
As waves shimmy, wrapping the sand,
The fish all giggle, share their thanks,
For life's great humor, hand in hand.

So laugh with the tides, let worries fly,
And roll with the waves, come what may,
For when echoes meet water, oh my!
The ocean's grin will brighten your day.

The Enchantment of the Wistful Sea

A crab in a tux with a bow-tie so neat,
Dances like mad on the slippery fleet.
He lost his cap, oh what a surprise,
While fish all around snicker and rise.

The seagulls are jesters, they dive with a flair,
Stealing a snack from a brand-new fair.
A whale plays the drums with his blubbery bass,
As jellyfish giggle, floating with grace.

A clam tells a joke, but it's quite the scare,
It sneezes on pearls that were just hanging there.
Shells cover their mouths, laughter erupts,
Even the barnacles join in the fun-ups.

So come, take a dip in this carnival wave,
Where creatures convene, so quirky and brave.
With gills full of giggles and fins full of cheer,
Each ripple a tale that will tickle your ear.

Melodies of the Everchanging Depths

A dolphin with shades swims to a tune,
He's holding a flute, making fish swoon.
An octopus jigs, with arms everywhere,
In this underwater party, without a care.

The bubbles are popping, the eels twirl about,
A sea cucumber frowns, just thinks it's a drought.
But then he decides to join in the beat,
Wiggling his way to the rhythmic sea sheet.

Starfish have come with their hands in a line,
To dance on the sand, feeling simply divine.
They twirl and they spin, although stuck to their rock,
Creating a show that's quite out of stock.

And when the tide shifts, they all tumble and roll,
Through water that sparkles like fun in a shoal.
With laughter and music, they wiggle and flip,
In depths where hilarity takes a sunlit trip.

The Last Drop at Dusk's Edge

A walrus in glasses, he's sipping some tea,
But it spills on a fish, oh dear, what a spree!
They both start to argue, a comical fuss,
While otters roll by, making quite the fuss.

The sun starts to set, it's quite the scene,
Where crabs change their hats with a twist and a sheen.
The shadows are long, as they gather for fun,
In this glow of the evening, the antics begun.

A pelican swoops, with a joke in his beak,
But drops it in seaweed; it's so bleak, so bleak!
But laughter erupts like a wave crashing down,
As a mermaid nearby wears a crown made of brown.

The hour grows late, yet they shimmer with cheer,
For moments like these bring the best of the year.
With splashy good vibes, they toast to the night,
As laughter and joy take an enchanting flight.

Epiphanies Beneath the Nautical Stars

A turtle named Tim with a vendetta for speed,
Wants to race with a fish, oh what a peculiar need!
With a wink of an eye and a splash from the tail,
They both dart away, leaving bubbles and trail.

A squid whispers secrets to shells by the shore,
While crabs draw up plans for a dance-off galore.
But one slips away, mysteries at bay,
As seahorses frolic in a funny ballet.

The anglerfish giggles, with a light on his hat,
Telling tall tales while playing with that.
With each little story, the moon gives a peek,
At the wonders of waters and time's funny streak.

And thus in the dark, under skies full of gleam,
Life flows like a current, a whimsical dream.
So raise up a glass, let's toast to the night,
For magic is real where the stars are so bright.

The Ballet of Seafoam and Silence

In a dance of bubbles, the sea sways,
Crabs take their bows in a comical craze.
The dolphins all chuckle, they leap and twirl,
While seagulls dive down, in a flappy whirl.

With foam on the floor, the tides take their cue,
A jellyfish prances, it's quite the view!
The starfish are giggling, they cling, they cling,
As clods of sand join for a beachy fling.

Oh, the waves do their jig, such rhythm and rhyme,
While seashells all clatter, they're keeping the time.
A mermaid rolls over, her hair all askew,
In a splashy ballet, the ocean's debut.

So watch as the humor unfolds with a crash,
For even the water can have quite the bash!
With laughter and frolic, the sea waves goodbye,
As pearly foam pirouettes under the sky.

Lagging Shadows on the Pier

Shadows pretend to be up to no good,
Stumbling on boards like they misunderstood.
The lighthouse winks down, amazed at the sight,
As seagulls steal snacks, flying off in delight.

The cat on the pier rolls, declaring his reign,
Ignoring the fish, he's part of the game.
With each little pounce, he is lost in his dream,
While ducks hold a meeting, all quack in a team.

The tide does its tango, the boats sway in glee,
Mischievous waves play, "Come join us, oh please!"
And fishermen chuckle at their empty nets,
As crabs skip around, placing funny bets.

So come, join the fun, on this creaky old deck,
Where shadows and sailors often play check.
With laughter and light, as the sun starts to chap,
The pier is a stage; it's a calamitous map.

Driftwood Dreams Beneath the Stars

Driftwood dreams whisper secrets at night,
While turtles debate if the moon is too bright.
A seal gives a nod and joins in the chat,
As jellyfish float by, all wobbly and fat.

Stars twinkle like coins, lost deep in the sea,
The crabs argue loudly about who won't agree.
With laughter and clatter, the night rolls away,
As sea urchins gossip till break of the day.

A long-lost sock drifts and claims it's a fish,
Saying, "Look at my fins! Just fulfill my wish!"
The waves raise their brows and nod with surprise,
As driftwood decides it can finally rise.

Beneath the vast canvas where dreams often play,
The ocean's own theatre puts on a display.
With snickers and splashes, it's never a bore,
As driftwood's grand dreams wash ashore evermore.

Nautical Murmurs of the Past

Hark! A ship bumbles, it's lost in the bay,
With pirates debating, "Should we sail today?"
Maps upside down, and the compass is wonky,
A parrot squawks loudly, "This tea tastes funky!"

Bubbles of history rise from the sand,
As mermaids dive deep, making hearts understand.
With giggles of sailors who made quite the fuss,
Their stories still echo, beneath the sea's bus.

Old anchors chuckle, as seabirds all squawk,
The echoes of laughter all dance and then walk.
The past plays a tune that the barnacles hum,
While fish pull a prank, and a sea turtle comes.

So join in the whispers, the jests with the breeze,
Where nautical nonsense flows with such ease.
In a whirl of amusement, the ocean will show,
That the past can be funny; just take it slow!

Ghosts of the Water's Reach

They dance atop the frothy sea,
With hats askew, how wild and free!
A parrot squawks, a seal goes, 'Boo!'
As jellyfish float and tug at you.

They tell of ships that lost their way,
With tales of fish who'd play all day.
Their laughter bubbles, a giddy sound,
While crabs hold court on sandy ground.

The mermaids giggle, tossing pearls,
While starfish play in whirl and swirls.
A sea cucumber's wiggly dance,
Makes even the octopus take a chance!

Gulls flap by with a cheeky caw,
As seaweed twirls without a flaw.
They tease the waves, they splash and dive,
In this funny world, we're all alive!

Phantoms Beneath the Moonlit Tide

With moonlight bright, the ghost fish gleam,
In underwater—a silly dream.
They serenade the night with jokes,
While laughing clams share silly hoaxes.

A lobster sings in opera style,
And even whales crack jokes with guile.
The bubbles rise, and spirits sway,
In moonlit fun, they dance and play.

A tidal wave of giggles spread,
As jellybeans float in ocean's bed.
The playful dolphins leap and spin,
With wink and nod, inviting in!

So raise a glass of seafoam drink,
And join the ghosts on the briny brink.
With bubbles up and laughter loud,
We're part of this whimsical crowd!

The Compass of the Wandering Waves

Sailing on a boat with wheels,
We steer through laughter and lunch-time meals.
With sandwiches lost to the salty breeze,
We keep on laughing, if you please!

The compass spins, it points and twirls,
As sea turtles dance and dolphins whirl.
We shout to gulls, 'Can't catch a ride!'
While shifting tides become our guide.

The siren's call is loud, yet sweet,
As gobs of sea foam tickle your feet.
The ocean sings with a cheerful glee,
While we hoot and holler, just you wait and see!

So sail along on this joyous quest,
With cap'n seagull, we're surely blessed.
Let's snicker at waves that splash our face,
In this funny frolic, we've found our place!

Secrets Cloaked in Ocean Depths

Beneath the waves, where secrets dwell,
An octopus spins a yarn to tell.
With ink and squirt, he takes the lead,
While fish roll on, they want to read!

A treasure chest filled with old socks,
And seaweed hats that rock the docks.
The treasures here, oh what a sight,
With giggles bubbling, it feels so right!

Nautical nonsense in every nook,
As plankton share the silliest book.
Anemones throw a flowing party,
For all the friends, both near and party!

So dive down deep for chuckles and cheer,
In the wackiest world, there's nothing to fear.
Let's dance with the shadows, laugh with the sea,
Underwater giggles, come and join me!

Shifting Sands and Echoing Footsteps

Upon the beach, the sun's a clown,
With footprints left, I chase them down.
I step in pits, I trip on shells,
My dignity? It surely dwells.

With buckets full of dreams to pour,
The waves retreat, then come for more.
I build a castle, grand and tall,
But seagulls think it's snack time call.

Oh silly wind, you twist my hat,
My hair's a tangle, just like that.
The tide is giggling, can't you see?
It's playing tricks and laughing at me.

Yet here I stand, a sand-made fool,
The ocean's jester, swimming in drool.
With every wave and splashy cheer,
I find my joy in salty beer!

Dreams Cast Adrift

I tossed my thoughts upon the sea,
They danced away, so wild and free.
With every wave, a wish goes high,
Maybe a fish will wave goodbye!

A paper boat floats by with grace,
It's carrying dreams with a silly face.
But strong winds laugh, and off it flies,
Leaving me here with soggy fries.

I tried to catch thoughts on a line,
But all I got was a crab, so fine!
He pinched my finger, what a mess,
Who knew wishes could cause distress?

With a wink, the sea calls my name,
It knows my heart but plays a game.
And when the tide pulls me away,
I'll surf on dreams, come what may!

Mooring to Endless Tomorrows

I moored my boat by the sand so bright,
But seagulls saw it and took to flight.
They stole my snacks, my lunch, my joy,
Now I'm left with just a toy!

The sunset laughs, a cheeky grin,
As I search for snacks that were once within.
The water sparkles, teasing me,
With thoughts of feasts gone out to sea.

A fisherman passes, with tales to share,
Of catching fish without a care.
But what's the secret? I want to know!
He just throws his line, and lets it go!

With each dawn, I will gather more,
And teach the tide some kitchen chore.
For in the dance of waves so grand,
There's always laughter, hand in hand!

The Serpentine Path of the Tide

The water's a trickster, it swirls and bends,
Leading my thoughts around the bends.
I walk the path of squishy mud,
With giggles trapped in every thud.

As crabs wave hello with claws held high,
I wave back, though I can't deny,
I stumbled then, and fell with style,
The tide just watched and cracked a smile.

The pathways shift like a silly game,
I chase a shell, but it feels lame.
Oh look, a starfish, it plays so dumb,
While I trip over kelp, much to my mum's.

In swirling water, laughter grows,
Life's but a dance with squishy toes.
So when the tide calls, I won't hide,
I'll ride the waves and claim my pride!

www.ingramcontent.com/pod-product-compliance
Lightning Source LLC
Chambersburg PA
CBHW071845160426
43209CB00003B/420